One Heart- Many Breaks
(A Collection of Poems and Art)

Sandeep Kumar Mishra

2

Remember

The poems are taken from the diary of the poet. Some poems are written when the poet was a boy, some when he was young man and rest when he became stoic to his adversity. Don't look for perfect language. They were not meant to be published. It's just the emotions and feelings at that particular times. All the originally is kept.

Awards And Honours

Amazon Best Seller Book
Readers Favourite Silver Medal
International Book Awards (ABF) Shortlisted
Indies Today Book Award Shortlisted
Literary Titan Book Award Shortlisted
New York Book Festival Shortlisted

Title-
One Heart -Many Breaks

Author –
Sandeep Kumar Mishra

Cover and other Art Work-
Sandeep Kumar Mishra

Illustration-
Hetal Mishra (Age-10)

Publisher
Indian Poetry Review Press

Edition-1/Aug 27, 2022

5

About the Poetry Collection

One sure thing in this life is that all of us will be disappointed somehow at some point. When we read or see someone with same fate we feel sympathetic or try to find solace in reading or talking about it. Same applies with this collection. The poems range in theme. Most of them are poetic reflections of personal emotions and situations he was laid in. The poems cover a 20 years life events and are expression of clear, true and purged feelings and stark reality of his situation. They also show his journey as a poet. More than half of the poems in the collection are published in different magazines in last 5 years in print or digital.

About the Poet

Sandeep Kumar Mishra is the poetry editor at Indian Poetry Review. He has received "Readers Favorite Award-21", "Indian Achievers Award-21", "IPR Poetry Award-2020" and "Literary Titan Book Award-2020". He was shortlisted for "2021 International Book Awards", "52nd New Millennium Award-2021", "Asian Anthology-2021" and "Joy B Poetry Prize 2021" and "Oprelle Poetry Prize 2021" and "MPT Story Award-2022' and 'Newcastle Story Award-2022" and "Anasi Story Award-2022".

More information -
https://www.sandeepkumarmishra.com/

**Acknowledgement-
Some poems have published before in these magazines,
journals or online-**

Society of Classical Poets, Third Wednesday, Blue Mountain
Review,Brasilia Review,Red Earth Review, Redfez, Reflections,
Scares,Snapdragon,Susan Journal,The Blotter, Criterion,Quail
Bell,The Human Touch,The Literary Yard,Thin Air,Torrid
Literature Journal,Willard and Maple,Winamop,Ygdrasil,Really
System,Poetry Soup,Asian Signature,Garfield Lake Review
Chiron,Review,Cold noon, Convergence,Curlew,Digging
Through the Fat,Down in the Dirt, Fixional,Good Men
Project,Poetry Nook Magazine,Harbinger Asylum,Hawaii
Review,Helix,High Plains Register,Joey & the Black Boots,
Literary Orphans,Marathon Literary Review,Phenomenal
Literature,ZOUCH Magazine & Miscellany,verbal art,London
Literary Review,San Antonio Review,Scene & Heard (SNH),
GFT Press,Bombay Gin, Stone Coast Review, Poetry
Space,International Times it, Poetry Leaves, Cardinal
Sins,Indiana Voice Journal,Mud Season Review, The Internet
Void,Salmon Creek,Dreamers Anthology,All Poetry,Canada
Quarterly, The Write Launch,DJ JELAL,Aquillrelle, Setu
Magazine, Rambutan Literary, The Bitchin Kitsch,Poetry on the
Move,Active Muse,Poem Village, Her Heart Poetry,Purcell
Press,The Fiction week, The Diary Files,Kuchh Poetic,The
writers and readers,Poem Hunter, Kitaab.Org, Poetry
Sydney,Realistic poetry,Able Muse,Poetry on the move,Tipton
poetry journal and many more.

My Life

Personal

Family

Society

I Painted an Ocean

I painted an ocean
but forgot the shore,
There were no ships,
When I took a close look,
it was my isolation sailing
like the sea waves.

I searched alone for centuries to
add the travellers in my voyage,
Still singular I stand on this mortal deck.
I need an island to anchor,
When I call on a radio,
It becomes silent monologue outward,
the reply comes from
the resounding empty inside.

With every tsunami from
the bosom of the core,
I feel like conulariid without pearls,
Although I have vastness of
Dead Sea but no light house
of life fervour.

My Gallery

In upper part of my body a cognitive bell rings
from a dial-up connection of live wires,
The modem is working just
to repeatedly provide the facsimile
of barren and bald family paths.

Inner lumbering of daily freight
coiling, clutching upward,
There is no vivacity,
the vital force has parasited,
How do I inhale life?

My days and nights are
bolted inside a brain cell,
My voice has held back,
It lays a plan to brawl my soul
residing in my own skull
and dictates notes imitating my tone
as I couldn't disintegrate my recall.

I see my sullen shadow has left me
There remains Just I, me and myself,
Why is my brain a black hole?
Could it not be a universe of
a constellation of migraine, tablets,
syringe, backache and insomnia?

My dreams have become a dead pattern
and as worn out as fossilized glow,
Everything has become identical except
the weight of consequence that
has variations of endurance.

As I go through perdition
my imbalance will be rectified,
Hang my remaining art on the wall
as after allotted time my gallery will end.

12

The Death of the River

My mental wire renders images
of worn out routes
after a short circuit happened
in the pathways of daily burdens.

My diseased body quivers with its
weight of hard- stitch, skin- snatched rubbles,
Leeched of life force as
I have little energy to breathe,
The voice I hear is not my own,
It dictates notes in familiar tones
but full of foreign phrases,
which it disguises as invitation.

I wish I could dissolve myself from
memory or hide in my skull cave,
but it is not wise to stifle,
Then an unlearned laughter came,
A spring emerges into the sun rays.
A sea emerges from the death of the rivers.
There are two ways to live a life,
I can pursue the difficult one.

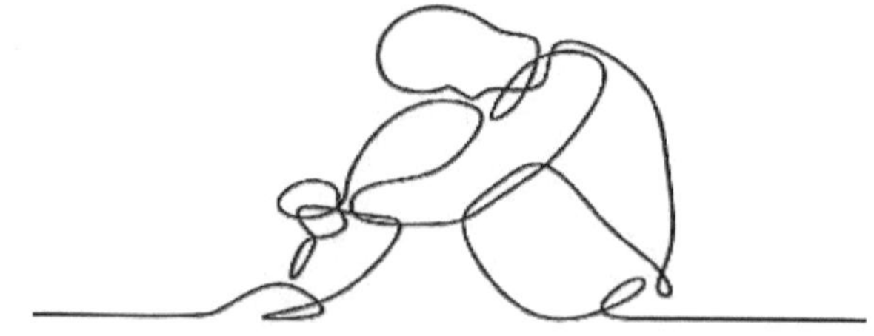

13

Bring Me More Pain

I want to see that ebony alter ego
that will take me to my doomed future
to see if there is break in the clouds.

No, No, wait! I have changed my mind
after some deliberations as it might
also show me the coming vicissitude
which I might not be able to face.

I will reconcile with my
torpedo dreams, spasmodic heart,
unfrequented nights, cantankerous days,
jaded body and harrowed soul.

Look ! Now I feel the perforated throb
in the middle of my heart when
life refuses to torture me.

Sip a Soul

I can only see on the black cloudy
shadow of infinity a delusion blathers,
A delusion of very existence,
A delusion of futility of mankind.

The glare of heavenly screen imparts
a persistent dementia,
In this state of insane superiority
morality becomes void as
opposite forms swallow each other.

I breathe pain,I breathe fear
I want to get that dark silence
where all forms get vanished,
Should I live to taste sins?

I don't have the courage when
I know it tastes bitter to
sip a fallen but sweet soul.

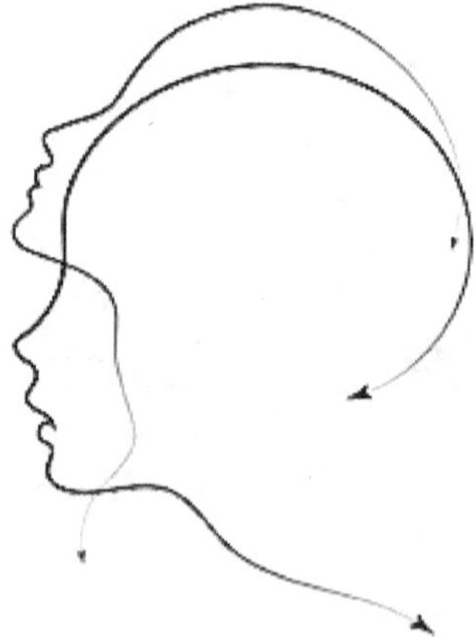

15

Sleep-On Sale

Every night I wander around bed- town
to buy some tranquil delights homegrown,
Dark ghostly mysteries of human life
persuade me to escape from
the day of struggle and strife.

I am eager to go that land of forgetfulness,
I track down that unknown territory but
can't find a way to make me weary,
When unfulfilled desires hover frequently
my fancy wide awake weaves his web brilliantly.

Sleep is a dream girl, a musk rose fragrance,
Melodies of a cookoo, the serenity of romance,
These beauties in bounty I always cherish
but every nocturnal errand will be quite garish
because sleeplessness has been my love interest.

Every day sympathies me but every night torments,
I am impelled to sell my reluctant sleep,
If anyone is willing to buy and ready to weep.

Why I Failed to Commit Suicide?

As we played curse of tongues so long,
in upper part of my chromatically complainant body,
a migraine bell rings from
a closed family dial-up connection.

My radio heart sometimes catches
the kind frequencies coming
out of my sputnik mother,
Personal road map is now offline,
as I go alone on worn out routes
with tolled lonely societal road
after so many accidents in
pathways of daily burdens.

All mechanic point disabled,
my transistor ability failed to switch innate
signals which my inner persona had,
The resistor mind failed to
terminate the wrong transmission line
my father and co put me in.

Faulty societal capacitor obstructed my path,
I couldn't store in me personal artistic energy,
as the negative economic charge
put my life to a disconnect,
Inner lumbering of daily freight of
earning a bread were coiling, clutching upward,
entangled my inherent dream of an artist
in closed circle of worldly obstacles.

They injected "delusion of negation"
in my blocked identity veins,
I although never had "flash flood of emotions"

I want to live by eating my chargrilled inner self.

Now a black hole, I decided to be one
with this constellation of migraine, tablets,
syringe, backache and insomnia that
had emerged around and bring apocalypse
in my life before that real cataclysmic
intervention by an outsider had an effect.

Planted on the old wooden chair,
looking at the ceiling fan,
I tied wife's red "sari" around
my disconnected neck,
I saw a reflection of my smiling daughter
in the mirrored almirah.
My brain waves dived low,
life swam across tumultuous oceanic heart and
my devil instinct drown into the deep
vastness of human frailty against
the coastal earthly emotions,
an inner tide hit me down unconscious.

That gave me one more label- A coward !
I can't even describe how angry
I was for not being among the dead,
The energy that I had to kill myself, is the kind of energy
I need to stay alive and I understood that.

The sun rays peeps through the dark cloud,
An ocean emerges from the death of the rivers,
There are two ways to live a life,
I can pursue the difficult one.

As We Stand in the Middle: A Need for Balancing Act

(What we got from Years of Self-Conceit)

A Letter to My Beloved Wife

Dear

If I could tell you anything or show you my heart feelings,that would have been a great make or break point of our life. But now I tell you by a medium that is media.

Although we have been living together as a married couple since 2003, ours is an unsuccessful marriage because we are not soul mates, even sometimes we act as enemies. Is it easy to love someone who doesn't love you back? Although we made a vow that we would indeed love each other. But it is a kind of "kickback love" which can't be called a love rather it is a business agreement.

One thing amazes me that we are still together. As you won't listen, I have portrayed my dilapidated soul suffering in the poems which I was writing for last three years. I have used some lines out of them to make you feel agony I have undergone.

"I want to see that ebony alter ego
That will take me to my doomed future
To see if there is a break in the clouds"

When I fell in love with you, I was raw and naive and got excited when you showed some interest in me. How do I know when I start liking a person if she will become an enemy for life? With the time the situation is becoming as such that has made me emotionally and physically weak.

When your raven-blown hair radiates—shades,
I repose in your lap, night comes, the day fades Your wondrous,
hazel eyes keep me at ease,
We will love till there are stars, skies, seas"

Are we so weak that we cannot pursue different paths or are we overly hopeful to get things sorted out one day? As we live in a small society and are bound by the traditions and may be some what fearful of the society, we are continuously suffering, but hesitant to break up in the hope that everything will be fine some day.

But this mismatch is wrongly affecting our two children. The situation has got better of me and I am going through the hell every minute. When I am upset, as is the case every other day, I don't interact and play with them. I have turned a bad daddy for them. Sometimes, even I slap them on slight errors. They are getting away from me. Why should these poor souls suffer because of no fault of their own?

"Is there a life beyond death?
Is there a path across the sky?
We are willing sinners,
But subject to a pardon"

Through this letter, I want to tell you that love is patient, love is kind. It does not envy, it does not boast, it is not proud. It always protects, always trusts, and always perseveres. Love is not self-seeking, the opposite of self-seeking. If we fall into the habit of loneliness, it will become our trait of life.

"I painted an ocean
But forgot the shore
There were no ships
When I took a close look,

It was my isolation
Sailing like the sea waves"

One reason for your resentment is my irregular job. I have proved a total failure on this front. As a temporary teacher, I could not manage my financial responsibilities well. Wrong investment and other gambles did not pay off. It has made the situation worse. Now I run in debt. I have to pay interest on them. I could not sleep at night. I have a migraine now.

The other part of the problem is that I always wanted to be a writer or a painter. But to be a successful writer, you need time and most importantly, money to make yourself famous by the use of modern social media and other publishing tricks and make some friends in the publishing fraternity as this is a subjective field.

I want to earn money by writing, but it is not easy and too late for me. I started to get published in 1994 but wrote only once in a while because of a troubled life since childhood. Sometimes there were gaps of 7 years between the articles.

"There is no vivacity
The vital force parasited
How I inhale life?
My days and nights are bolted"

Now the situation is such that I fear to return home, as a nag-fest waits for me behind the front door. I have thoughts to talk my feelings, but in the back of my mind, I know that you won't either listen carefully or not going to understand it completely.

So it is all inside just burning hole, making me resentful. You have an aggressive tone of voice and posture. Day and night taunt me with some kind of sarcasm or ridicule. Sometimes we don't speak at all. I am in a constant duel with my inner self, but blaming outer resource for a defeat.

"Every night I wander around bed- town
To buy some tranquil delights homegrown,
Dark ghostly mysteries of human
life persuade me to escape
From the day of struggle and strife,
I am eager to go that land of forgetfulness,
of that unknown territory"

As you are unaware my unhappy childhood has made me so reactive. Do you have time and heart to know my background? This flashback will help you to understand my weaknesses.

We have to develop a mechanism to resolve the matter and it will save us from more years of helplessness in our marriage. Anyone could have unsuccessful marriage, but a good level of adaptation for some good and bad reasons is necessary.

"Why is my brain, a black hole?
How could it not be a universe
of a constellation of a migraine, tablets,
syringe, backache and insomnia?

How can we call ourselves a married couple when we don't sleep on the same bed or in the same room? I want to sit with you, pour my heart out to you, make love to you, enjoy a dinner with you at some restaurant, and go on a trip.

But all these things have become a dream; In fact, when I see other happily married couples, more often than not, I feel tormented. I haven't attended a party or visited a friend for a long time. I rarely go market. I don't socialize. I even don't dress properly as you see and told me many times.

"My mental wire renders
Images of worn out routes,
After a short circuit happened
In the pathways of daily burdens,
My diseased body quivers with its
weight as it is leeched of life force"

When a person is sad, the world seems nothing to him. Whom he would get dressed for? Don't you feel a bit for me? During the day, I consciously remain busy as I try to keep a distance from you. But this is also having a negative effect on my eyes and back as I sit 10-12 hours continuously on the computer.

On the other side, when you are free, you think to talk, discuss, or entertain yourself with me, but we are so cut from each other that no one has the courage or humbleness to step up first.

"I will reconcile with my
Torpedo dreams,
Spasmodic heart,
Unfrequented nights,
Cantankerous days,
Jaded body
And harrowed soul"

I want to start afresh. We have to lift ourselves. We have to leave our egos aside. Many times I think to make some simple affirmations like when I go home, I will see my children and wife or we will have a good time together. But it does not happen. I need your help.

Every morning we should claim a wonderful day by giving thanks or praise to each other for some work. You will feel an energy flowing within. It is biblical to say that no weapon against you will prosper, but it is human to believe that people are out to take from you.

"When faith is bright, doubts loose lustre,
When wisdom grows, the tears shrink;
Every bough waits for bloom to bring,
Hope gives you chance of second spring"

You can pinpoint your views, but the tone should be cooperative.
So accept differences and make them opportunities.

"The body of Christ has different parts that
come together in unity"

The simple solution is to look in my eyes and say, "You are not
my enemy". I am introvert but will try to show it now and then.
Would some little gestures, touches, and gifts or it may be a
picnic, a film a shopping time do the good?

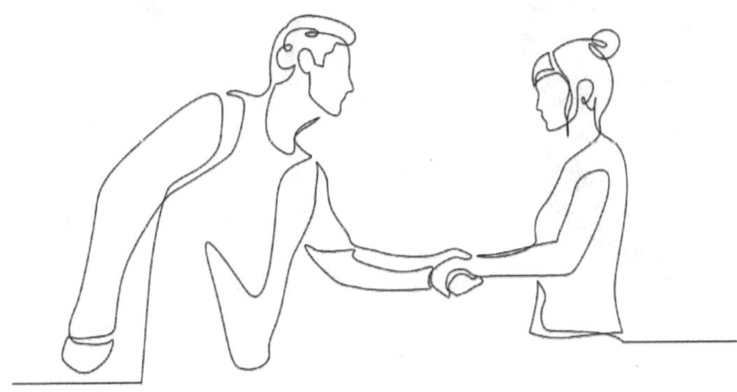

A Tree in My Courtyard

A momentous tree in my courtyard
The only heritage, I received, a bard.
The iridescent leaves with dainty blossom
Sweet upshots bounty, some retired jetsam.

I listen twitching eerie chirrup from
the playful sparrows' faggot home.
A joyful jump every sunup it whispers me up
As dry leaves surge like sweet syrup.

I stand beneath to duplicate the persona
A morn breeze sweeps like a drink yagona.
My lady kindles lamp fuelled with a hymn
She touches rugged feet to take some blessing.

Whenever dejected, I always locate him
His soothing voice but in a mime.
All the afternoon it meditates like a hermit
My wise elder brother I must admit.

Every eve juveniles play in shadow
Ripe sweet fruits what they endow.
My dark bed is in his yard
I sleep like his darling ward.
There remains no discerned gap
As I dwam in his hazy lap.

Seascape

My love, my dream! Come with me
We will blanket the lea, beyond the sea.
Build a palace among the stars
Far from earthly strife and wars.

Look at the rainbows, the white rivers
Slaty mountains, red roses, brown sparrows.
Bright glow worms, golden eagles, black bees
Yellow sunflowers, scarlet macaw, green trees.

Showers drench morning, nights glow with dew
Posy noon to dose, then evening linnets in view.
Winter with warm sun, moonlit cool nights
I admire thy grace, thy touch razes my frights.

When your raven-blown hair radiates—shades
I repose in your lap, night comes and day fades.
Your wondrous, hazel eyes keep me at ease
We will love till there are stars, skies and seas.

27

She Walks in Rhyme

When my eager-eagle eyes saw thee,
I found a thrall in the veins.
A stop in the labor heart pumping the red,
Like a day of golden sun in summer bright.
She comes as morn's refreshing breeze,
Seems a living garden forever in bloom.

Half shy of her own glory,
Fair than the fairer, a shine that never fades,
Her aspects best of dark and light.
Her lips are coral red and
Cheeks are roses red and white,
A valley in the breasts, deep and steep
A smile that wins a thousand realms.

Her charm that pleases but
Might waste thy youth in sighs.
Her airy hair swings spider' silver line,
Mild voice fades like an old opera tunes,
The perfume of her soul feels in your vigour,
As she walks in rhyme on blank verse path,
A thousand nameless graces move.

When she dances with autumn leaves
Some soft whisperings vibrate in our spirit.
She shakes earth beneath and sky above
For she is a deity, an incarnation,
I can only see through my close eyes.

A Flash Fiction

An unacquainted damsel inhibited
my way the other day,
As a musk deer leapt,
A moon came out of dark cloud.

Face, half covered with raven tresses
switched on night in the day,
Her style and grace were heavenly,
I urged my instant proposal,
She sulked,vanished away
Like a bubble in water.

This flash meeting
An anecdote for life,
I can't voyage her trail
In this worldly sea,
but would inspire a bard
being intellectual fellow henceforth.

A Rainbow Memory

When my hollow present blows
the dying embers in the heart grate,
a fond childish cinder glows up.
The frozen black memory melts past colours,
A sparkle of rainbow recollections,
As I walk up on our trodden pavement
I saw a slash of sea between houses.

Thy red dress like a bright red boat
sinks in golden sand,
I catch blue fishing nets,
Paint those brown fort walls
at green lichen beach.

My soul speaks, my lips moves
A frequency of meetings, a wave of hugs,
As I net to catch these moments
like a street urchin's yellow fists
holding the rainbow in his tiny grasp.

My Mother

Since she left me for a long journey,
every day my clock starts with zero
but there is no zero on other clocks.
I don't know where my mother lives,
Previous night my skin felt soft as
she kissed with her wet lips.

My mother wished to see me upbeat,
she replies about her recent minor
emergencies about her well being,
about how she played with my siblings,
she needs me to return to life.

I wonder why only humans need to
figure out how to move with reason?
Is that why we nag rationale?
It's been simple not to go there,
I know I should meet her but
My past burdens stop me
to meet her in her promised land.

My Father

My father never did womanly things
like taking his kids in his lap and
loving or playing with them,
Yes, he did masculine things of breaking
some mirrors,hitting the doors or
his head against a wall,
slapping his children and abusing
everyone when helplessness trapped him
in the web of poverty,tension
and unfulfilled desires.

Orthodox and religionist in him taught us
most superstitions that made him a sage
devoid of social life and me almost an atheist.
He taught us good values without
letting us in his room.

We had seen him write poems
but we were not part of his universe,
The world may be familiar with his works
but we haven't read his books as
we have developed immunity to it.

As a private school teacher, he changed many schools
as his straightforwardness disliked by admins and
his honesty out casted him to attend any
social gatherings or functions.

He didn't tell us our history or geography,
Oblivious of siblings, locked in a closed family circle,
Ignorant of our community,
we live at the borders of our social circle now.

I wish to be with my father, talk,learn
and serve him but still I lack a bond,
I haven't seen him for long time and
never feel a need or pain of it.

He is counting his time,
his legacy some published books
and unpublished manuscripts
lying in a store almirah,
The long gap between us stops me
to take those few steps,
it seems a long journey.

Upbringing and luck shape our life,
my father was child of his misfortune and
I am child of my father.

33

My Sister

From those innocent years when
we shared our lives together,
I remained deeply attached to you
more than I did to our mother.

When we had to be apart,
you went to your house,
Still I was with you like a dowry,
I spent my younger days with you
as my brotherly love was at
your service in sun or rain.

You always think of me first,
You have supported me,
have known me deep inside,
but still so many things, I hide.

There came a time when a thunder struck,
We took our individual ways but
if only you have told me my fault
It would have been a better apart.

When you failed to meet me on that "Raksha day",
it proved our bond was too sweet to
sustain in a long life run,
I wonder perhaps our love was a bubble
or the moment took better of us.

Still you know what I desire,
All the misunderstandings and silly fights
that made us sad, is part of growing up,
You taught me so many lessons of life,
the good, the bad and the meaning of strive.

34

I was ignorant of worldly ways,
Here a poor soul is thing to ignore,
you were dwindling between
various family relationships
so my love's labour lost in financial battlefield.

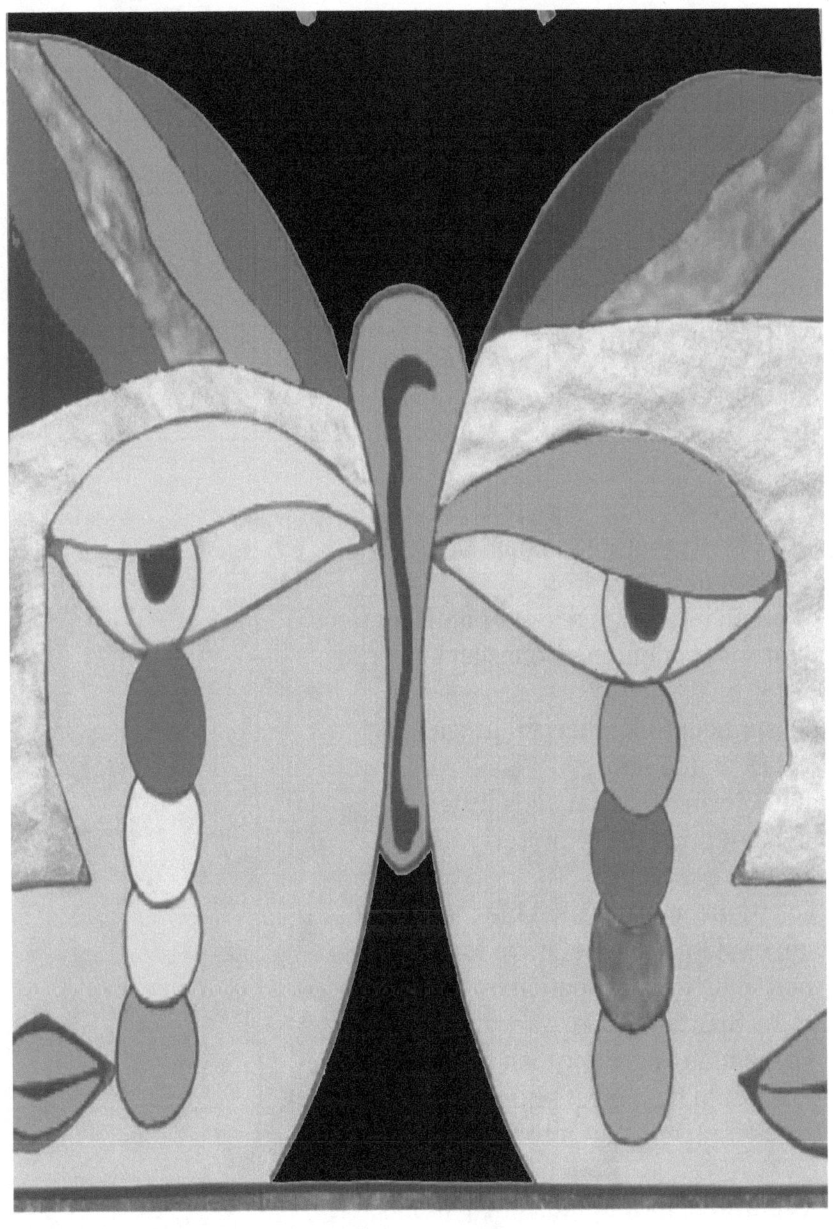

A Visit to Hospital

Hospitals are ideogram of truth
where death has no false tint of life-
pukka pain, pink anguish but stained hope.

You might see Hoag's a galaxy
within a galaxy within a galaxy
One patient, like phoenix,
obtains new life by arising from the ashes
but other dies in a show of
flames and combustion malady.

It's white walls has deserted
its real petro- aromatic daughter,
to adopt new step aroma
of medicine,syrup, dettol or antiseptic
with some odourless bones and meat.

It's surgical folk, cheerful green,
with fear and hope
in the form of dream adds little
love potion to every prescription.

The ill are so true pale blue that
you could not but be brave to see
these patients with patience
of the Spartan school,
As the man is greater than his pain,
you would be a great philosopher,
once you come out of this stoic building.

A soulful comes to meet the patients,
Holding a hand, you feel like your house keys in hand,
but here no heart is by-passed by love,

When you hug them their ribs make
a room for your fleshy abdomen,
as you sense the titanic waterfall
of their hearts slowly sinking.

Avoid any mirror or self reflection,
You won't see the things you usually
see but your purged soul will peep out
of body fabric like the sun light
coming out of a barred window.

It is hard to balance petty yourself as
inner burden will be more than the body weight,
Let us praise these insomniac beds,
let us praise the fans that do not adjust,
praise the room service that doesn't exist,
let us praise the hospital staff
they are angels without wings.

Covering under fake mask of joy
they find expired lungs and tired hearts
lying in their paths every day,
They play poker with their lives
in this game with virus and ailments,
fostering death for other passive parties too.

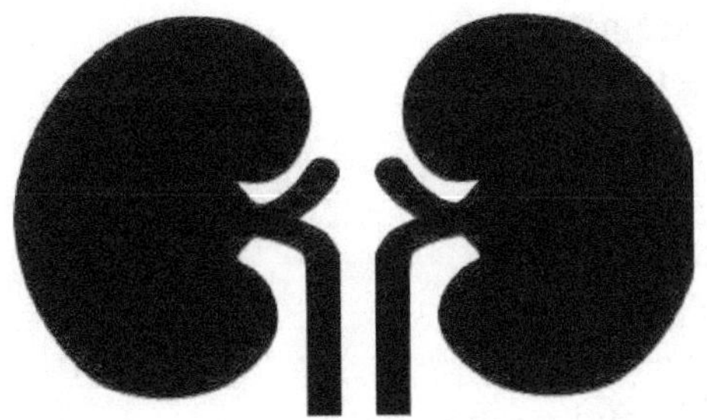

Corona -Vorona Days-Ways

Humanity is caving in corona motion,
I am as sea mouse back to my hide-hole,
An alarm every morn, but remain in bed to ignore,
What seems like minutes are hours,
Week and weeks spent in hibernation,
Am I a little lonely bear?

Homesick in my home
put in non Covid-19 home jail,
It feels a creepy clown chasing me or
I am being cornered by zombies,
I work from green home in red zone world.

Log on for socialising, switch on to remote voice,
My body robots repeat eat, sleep and eat.
Is breakfast still breakfast if I have it at 12 ?
Is dinner still dinner if I have cookies for tea?

I blink my eyes, focusing in on the horizon
as if concentration will transport me there,
Did I just see a butterfly land in that flower?
When kookaburras flying over empty streets,
Do they know what is happening to us?
Am I noticing more than I did before?

As lungs feel clear, birds are now planes,
we venue out of the house to
the garden and back in again,
it's made all of us hermits.
The sky is blue now, or is it just me?
Now I understand less means more.

Relentless panting of traffic and people

is now marathon conscious breath,
We shop to track down others health,
Sanitizer in the pockets with face masks,
Sneezing is a way to attract attention now,
Corona warriors are on the front line
but some people still curse and cry.

This thing is non-fiction- health vs economy,
Even the fiction is dark, but there's still music,
Covid-19 is a hydra- headed challenger
to our modern modality to wake up
buying cheap tack from cheap labour.

I wonder why I feel a sense of guilt
when I see others suffering while I am not,
I am now getting used to my pyjamas.

My City

My city enjoys a mugged face
Malls- skyscrapers connect its vital limbs.
The days ejects laborious force
as nights being stiffly precarious climbs.

Horns, siren, music, pollution, buzz and silence
beat a million drums to compose dumb sounds.
Burgeon heads grow at every empty place
to take the junta of humanity its daily rounds.

These burghers never stop but wriggle a lead
Ten to five, incessant flinty work culture.
There is light around, but scenery seems fade
targeted digging out life becomes grave for nature.

Feeble morn walker or greasy evening wanderer
Mechanical late sleepers or impotent late risers.
Sofa, carpet, TV, mobile and air conditioner
All are granite museums but no drowsy reposer.

High ways are the death ride way
I strive for a peaceful lee.
Has city ruined me in any way?
No, it has marred better men than me.

I stand alone amid a million crowd
God was silent when I was suffering fast.
I am not ready to die ignored
I'll build a new city before I breathe last.

City Life

Bright delights but dull life
Hustle –bustle, chaos and strife
Way to thrive, a mechanical life
Most artificial, less nature
One society, mix culture.

Hot concrete but cold steel
Many sympathies, but few will feel
Many laughs but some will smile
Disco, pub, hotel and club
Fun and frolic, city is the hub.

Lots of thorns, a few roses
Fake friends but real foes
Yours joy and your woes
Small families but little hearts
Big walls but small gates.

Most are unknown, some are familiar
Future is uncertain, present is clear
All are distant, a few are near
City has various prospects
A lot of fiction, few are facts.

Long to go, little to get
Few will act but many react
Some gives but many will take
No penny on an edge of the knife
Luck in your side, a lavish life.

Few are wise, the most are smart
All are mature, few are innocent
A race to run, don't get outsmart

42

When you ride, don't look aside
Long journey, but the gap is wide.

I, my, for me is the only notion
Lots of motion, zero emotion
Bounty of pain, but few are potion
Sofa is mountain, Carpet is the sea
This is the city made for me.

****

Mini Poems

1
The breast-feeding mother
is not shameless,
she is shameful In her affection

2
The "Khajuraho" art is not obscene,
that's beautiful scenery
in its observation

3
Modern man is not nude,
he is un- naked
but in his fashion-mood

4
The man is not animal,
he's human
but in his material performance

When You Buy Their Sorrow

Icy winds filled with chimney smoke
signals the burning of Christmas block,
When colourful lights all around gleam,
the holy monks sing the merry theme.

Sacred lilies and decorative ivory fill homes
Town to town our joyful echo roams,
Perch like a bird around the trees to sing
Listen to chorus, sweet jingle bells bring.

Meet the beloved ones you missed daily
Hug the foes,don't let slip away easily,
Rich and poor at the same table
Do the labor but make it a fable.

Let care go some hidden place
Let love take its due space,
Drink and drown your worry
No one seems alone or in hurry.

Once you have the Christ sign in thy heart
Feeling His grace makes you Gilbert,
The God loves all in their true form
Shun the bad habits in His charm,
Time to wish all a prosperous morrow
It's Merry Christmas
when you buy their sorrow.

Symbol of climax!

Beyond man
All creatures swallow one another
Due to their mental senselessness,
But today man eats man,
Is it bankruptcy of his wisdom
or symbol of climax!

We Are Third World

Self acclaimed first world nations
labelled us as third world in their
so called socioeconomic indexes and
other "modernity is the real development" indices
because we don't do dinner parties
but dream of a well fed day.

Our children study on the floor of old public school,
know the other world by the greenery
and figures hung on its pale walls,
They wish to run on the velvet grass
instead of rag picking every morn,
As children leave old toys,you have abandoned us.

Here a teenager gets mature in his teens
and recognises outline of a dark futuristic
structure in a pattern of present dots of daily burdens,
In the tragic repetitions of a homeland song,
he dreams of a young entrepreneurship
but a termite death hollows out his roots of endeavour.

You say to our men"Keep It In Your Pants!"
and women, "Lock Your Knees!"
but here sex is the only amusement,
for a three minutes of relief we are ready
to repent and live life of corruption and immorality.

Although some taxable souls fashion to run charity,
the poor wears tattered clothes,
rich wear them to look different,
There is an agreement between the person
sitting in the car and poor begging for some help.

Devalued lives full of shadows of slaves
as poverty live without evacuation,
Caught in web of the foreign aid spiders,
we prop up this capitalising protuberance
and force feed the bourgeois class,
Our propaganda has become just
to see,sigh and cry.

Blindfolded by civil war,
a source of political life and death,
we fail to understand the kind of battlefield
we are in and our weapons to deal with it,
Always shouting for freedom of expression,
never tried to know the difference
between our skin and our lips.

A divided country that sighs and cries for debt relief,
is brainwashed by anti-propaganda,
As leaders becoming millionaires every second
and the people poorer every minute,
the land filled with milk and honey,
still cries "no money"

Self styled media with fake morality,
aiming for PR and controversy interview
a petty thought repeatedly to make it a philosophy,
their voice spreads pure venom in gentle dress,
in the name of so called minority,
every news is labelled with religious stamp,
they highlight the immoral as a face of nation,
belittle the good-intentions.

Sex and violence is a new form of entertainment,
here big lawyers and corporations openly influence
in the demo-crazy capitals to gain huge profits,

Is this injustice with poverty and
suffering not a clear indication of false thoughts
that argue over a third world at this juncture.?

****

This Age –Air

New –creation ?
Any selfless offering? Some dedication?
No! Quite not.

Now the social valuations are varied
They stand still at the core of wealth,
So only money-making,
All around Wonga-wish.

Oh! this is age –air
"Penny –chaser" has no fear.

49

Soap Opera

Our life is a god-sponsored opera as
we daily shoot for worldly advertisement,
A daily melodrama in which an individual
episode has a rotation of story-line,
An episode may end, but the story never ends,
There is chance, missed opportunities,
Sudden conversion, last minute rescues,
We rehearse our allotted part but someone
is always there to replace.

Every relay has a new story,
Some have easy, some complex plots.
Our roles are not our choices,
You may be tragic or comic but
the truth-the play will entertain the folks.
Sometimes we do the same role
to be labelled as buffoon or villain.

As I have stereotyped in tragic role,
No one is willing to offer any other role.
Now it is not important If I am pleased or not
I must take the standpoint of the director
and finish my part.

To Be Modern

New age illusion -
"To be modern"
What we get?
"A run in a circle"

What remains?
"A tortured soul,
and hollow body"

And
"No bridge to take
ahead or back"

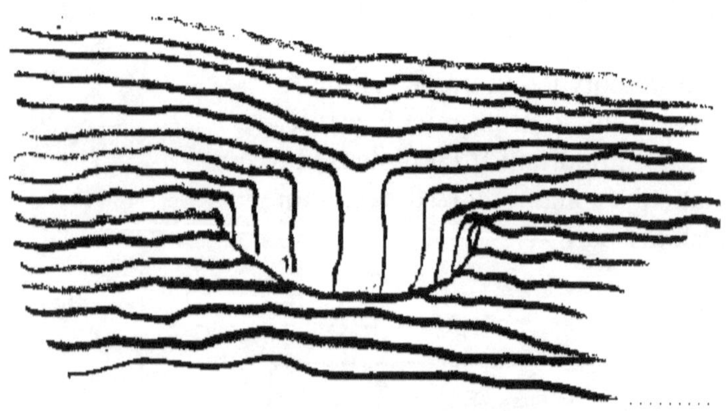

51

The Reality

Why are we shocked with the space we owe
and convey with it a specific frustration?
How little we need to bring
that main exhilaration that exists.
Is this the exhilaration we've carried with us?
I wonder not a single companion is with us.

Frangipanis outside needs thy steady acclaim,
The inflated shafts, once a primary fascination,
looks fit for somebody other than me,
Still it's mine now and I think will be known
by the art I hang on the wall.

May be that is the reason wherever we
go nowadays vanity has tailed us like a pet.
But when we believe in anecdotes than
worldly companions can never be ours.

I feel that with a house this way,
I should set up a major gathering
that would please with vulnerabilities
of night and simply attempt to settle in
as everybody even in his own space,
is a vexed visitor.

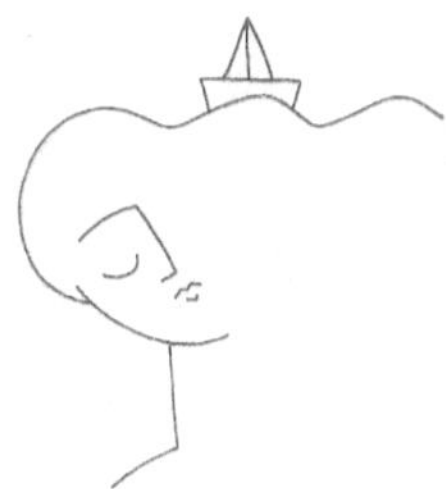

The Books

Books are in restless wintry mood and
their voices seem urgent,
What the books whisper, we prefer not
to mention in social circles,
Yet they know more and have been where
we can't go in the clothes we wear.

They are unsettled, we are motionless,
Their voices are foreign to our ears.
They disdain, they will shake us off,
Too many voices, too many lost conversations.

When I open a page and fall into
its frosty profundities to sink
like a stone, I talk in cliches.
They hover in time like bad omens and
flap wings as their frantic pages cloud the sky.

They are the darkness in our bones
that keeps on sparkling like dead flames.
What a struggle they endure day and night!
Some books unopened stay to sight,
Books of some pasts have been scorched
or may long live not a page turned.
To die unread of ripe old age or
by next generation earned.

Yellowed-book-worms devoured in rage!
There's a thing common— books or men,
but a few significant can discern.
Every book has its shining creed
which we fail to read and believe.

Pebbles

Time smooths rainbow hardness of tree basalt,
vermilion jasper, silvery granite and
pale feldspar with the help of humdrum
but patient jeweller of tides.

Volcano-born, earthquake-quarried,
heat-cracked, wind-carved,
death shapes compact among the rocks,
It drifts light as a fractured bone.

When the tide uncovers,
it blinks among the smashed shells.
Upset by gulls, bleached by salt and sun
the broken crockery of living things.

An eagle surveys from the upland,
unsympathetic to the burdens
I have carried here,
The sea would not hug me,
so I sit, hollow as driftwood,
jumbled as pebbles.

O Stars!

When I goggle at the screen
of wild black yonder,
O stars! I feel a blazing avidity
in my vital limbs.

Elan eyes of the angels,
invested in with thousand finesses,
show your cloudless sparkle to
the ignorant world.

The magnetic star adjacent the moon
guides the sailor way out.
My heart responds to thy
flickering with life
and ignites my bituminous soul
with an immortal spark.

56

First Monsoon

Immigrant pregnant clouds in this high time
preparing to deliver aerial showers.
Huge watery vessels, like a developed baby
Too heavy to hold in atmospheric womb.

With lightening proclaiming over
the vastness of the supply of life fluids,
Weary peasants' restless eyes wait for
their intimate dark relatives.

Timorous honeybees, humble sparrows at bowers,
Come ! welcome the procession of yearly joy
and acquire this treasure of wet stuff.
Silvery tip-tip deepens every available aide,
Pure life distils from the lofty branch- let,
A pacy white perennial stream is on a raid.

Polished jade vegetation, rinsed pavement is wet,
Everything is tame now, the wild gets modest.
The sweet scent of sand is tempting to taste,
I want to be wet party, some memento to keep.

Watery pearls blush their face in late Sun rays,
Feathered creatures in row, rainbow crescent sways.
Candour heart inhaling aromatic worship,
The earth colourfully adorned like an Indian bride
In her first monsoon, commanding pride.

Divine Dusk

The pale elderly sun looking back
through the holes of warm mountainous gap
toward his legacy which he owned
and enjoyed in his nubile time.

Those worldly parceners
are preparing for a new morrow,
The birds, homeward, in a row
like a bow aimed at the twilight sky.

Slow lowing herds measure tired trails
as herdsmen plod their weary way.
The dust clouds mask the air
In this sphinx inky time.

Holding a glimmer of eve lamps
the trees erect ghostly figures.
Look! The premature early "Hesperus"
with his twin, a half crescent moon,
A delicate image with starry background.

When sun touches his westerly abode,
wise interact on a stony –round banyan.
Faint church bells in spiritual broadcast
airs the tenure of mortal industry.
This is divine dusk time,
Reminding the inevitable to you-
A feeble mankind!

Winter

In snowy unpigmented drape
wintry withdrawn world waits
for the warm kiss of the day.
Through the long lonely valley
the elevation blows the glacial gale
to cheer the deep and solemn solitude.

Over the bare upland, a pious sunbeam
plays when the heartless west extends its blast
but the stormy north sings sleet.
All the field lay bound beneath
a crispy integument of snow,
It withers all in silence to expose the earth
and show its susceptible skeleton life.

I walk to crash crunch beneath my feet
to see a dancing darkness in vivid blue.
In an ecstasy the earth drinks
the lukewarm silver sunlight.
The beast or bird in their covert rest,
These leafless trees resemble my fate,
as a lonely robin with its burning breast
sits in subtle sweetness of the sun.

How ruby banner of poppies spread
where the lilies fell asleep but
the rose's hearts are beating still.
When the fresh sap of earth
finesse the flaxen flowers,
The snowflakes swarmed in the yard
to beat the feeble window panel.

When, I step in warm chamber,

I wonder how like me
the grief worn threshold stone was?
Distorted and shivering shadows are
upon the dim lighted ceiling.
The colourless clusters of lacklustre stars
ornaments the night bride.
The lenient liquid moon slides
through bare black branch.

A chamber corner draft swept the night stand,
The cruciform contour of winged craving
took a fleety flash flight,
I swear to keep every sweet promise
under a warm furry blanket of seed prospect.
God pity all those homeless souls.

My Cottage

My cottage, an idyllic allure, shimmers
in the morning sun beneath semi-liquid cyan skies.
With hiss of long snake pavements,
silky dark green lawn greets me when
I come from my daily grind.

I feel the thrust of flying feet,
eager to reach my seraphic habitat.
Whenever dejected, there is always
its approachable inspirits walls.
The roof is a shield against moody forces,
All rooms are the measures of leisure,
Oxygenated windows broadcasting outer view.

It relaxes in the evening shadows when
a small bird perches on the sill,
On eventide, I sink to dreamy slumber
oblivious of the realm of human experience
reclining on a deep pillow.

61

Morning Ecstasy

Reluctant night slowly retreating,
Grey earth, some dim shades still hovering.
Dawn strides out leisurely to wake every farm
Sleepy sun with liquid light make the sand warm.

Morning nymph rising from the ocean
of pearls wearing magic mist mantle
as the wind swirls her gleaming bracelet.
Borrowed from sun rays swiftly up to
the hilltop her glory sways.

Her fragrance wakes up the slumbers of mortals,
The crowing birds but break the silence acetals.
I am eager to rise early than the bee,
Perhaps to feel the divine power if it be.

Every home kindles its necessary fires,
Sense morning incense, listen far sounding lyres.
The soul feels fresh and rejuvenated as
healing light exhaled a divine incarnated.

The bunches of roses and the lily awaken,
The wind hides in trees, make them shaken.
Shy maid advances with pitcher to fill in river,
The peasants and herdsmen on their way as ever,
All creatures must toilsome courses run hard
Because untrodden the path, bright is the reward.

Hope

When a night liquidates a day
as a sinful cloud plasters its sun,
all ticklish bonds fade away
to make every assemblage a ruin.
Despair sits like a gloomy owl
when destiny becomes our foes.
Heavily barred body entrap
the soul with bowed head and lowered eyes.
If no one quaffs thy soulful drop,
Say yoo-hoo in the piper called hope.

All treasures can be taken away
but can't rob thy hope.
A hundred universes have sway
but only thy heart makes its scope.
Hope perches in like a kite
only sings when you cry.
If there is dearth of light,
Its gold mine dug in thy yard.
Remember after a wailful black night
day breaks wondrously clear bright.

Soar not too high, skies are tall
and the stormy clouds are near,
They press you back for a great fall.
Remember, when hope falls no one hears,
the stocky ruin is within to clear.

If running out of hope, you can borrow
It is a timid friend, cruel in his fear.
Intimating thy sorrow, delivering a new morrow,
Every bough waits bloom to bring,
Hope gives you a chance of second spring.

The After Effect

Why is it necessary?
A row of lights when we supposed to sleep?
Colourful neon fantasies when we dream?
Using intoxicants to slow our breath
when we should be panting with labor?

Why are there two personalities?
When we have our shadows.
Yes, they call it progress or may be
it is another name for self-destruction.

We intentionally suspend ourselves between
the seas and the skies while
we have the earth beneath our feet.
We grow the fruits of antithesis
on the false trees of thesis
while there is rich land of synthesis.

As we stand among the crowd to
feel the ease of empty space,
Perhaps we can hear the whispers
of stars and planets with
only after dead ear to humanly voice.
All travelling this flaky pious life
with the pack of lies, each face is filled with
its own far away death wrinkles.

We count billion to consecrate
the hour in only single digit as
our consciences strive to be true.
Is it sensible emptiness while
we long to drink the pure mirage?

Every heart is dipped in dark India ink
as the sky nurses on black milk.
The earth trembles with its movement as
do the Chance, Beauty and Youth with
burden of fear and hope of labor and play.

A poet is also part of this dilemma,
If a poem becomes an enigma,
If a poem does not offer a solution,
Don't read or look at it otherwise
it will affect you like an after effect of
a wrongly prescribed medicine.

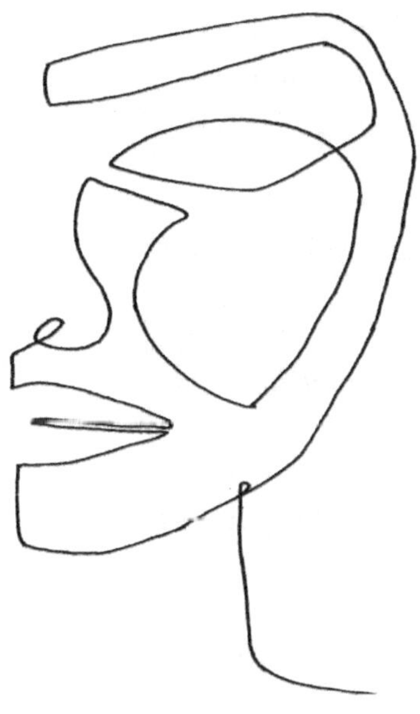

De-branched or Not?

They say going away is but
an initial of creation be it a big bang
or a garden fruit, when they
are ripe or ready, they are de-branched.

But I prefer a simple union,
not a detached one
because avalanches waits for
those who strays far and wide,
Then half of the life is wiping
the other half for cleaning.

While going off is part of the process,
Why is this division or decrement?
One part detached, one part united,
How dispersal changes into sweet attraction!

It is a wireless connection with
relationship at various levels which
we would love more but forget completely.
As the distance defines the correlations,
We will meet but misfortune suffices.
A refuge for the time,
It is not the matter of gain or loss as
a joy kindles the sadness of separation.

Voice Within

As the evil is sire of morality,
As the night toe the line of a day,
The clouds may be dark –heavy
but only they can bring the rain.

When faith is bright, doubts loose lustre,
when wisdom grows, the tears shrink.
Is there a life beyond death?
Is there a path across the sky?

We are willing sinners but subject to a pardon,
When a path closes for you,
the other is always there beforehand.
When you hear a voice within,
its purity of soul, faith in yourself.

Enjoy the Sun Energy

Does in the dark realms of the past
the present throw a light?
When the sharp painful realities pinch
a life does the past relieve us?
Thinking of the tomorrow
deprive you of the inherent,
unseen tiny joys of stressful present life.

Develop the insight,
enjoy all the elements
while they are present.
Feel the sun energy while it is there
because the night is not far behind.
In search of new flowers,
Don't go away from your roots,
Don't lament a past or strive for
future because today is the day.

Beauty: Beatitude

Beauty is blessedness and an euphoria,
When life unveils her holy face,
Some soft whisperings speak in our spirit.
The eternity gazes itself in a mirror,
It glows with pure tints of varying hues.
It shall rise with the dawn from the east,
As a lock of angels forever in flight.

Exulting beauty descends from centred
and from errant sphere a balmy nectar glows.
Its enchantment entices the bosom,
Come! See the breezy dome of groves,
As its fountain quench the thirst of magic thrall.

Forget Me Now

When I breathe last,
Don't weep at my grave or inscribe
a stone for I won't be there.

Death is slave to the luck,
Nothing it could do.
I will change my form,
My ashes will be one with
the crust of the earth,
I would revolve with its
diurnal path and be live
again for forever, eternal I become.

For me, life would mean all
that more than If ever meant whatever,
You can afford to forget me now.

Descending into the Earth

Death unescorted by feet or form,
Difficult to trace bare bone footprint.
Discern its image in the mirror of vitality,
Its spirit draws breath in the body of life.

Death is interior of the slushy flesh,
Trial-mount on the funeral pyre
to feel the body fabric burning.
You're not descending into the Earth
but rising towards the eternal Sky,
and entering a pristine nativity.

As the Sun sets, the Moon rises.

72

That Nice Elderly Year

That overhasty elderly year is
lying on his death bed which was
a fellow of our previous paths and
a willing caller to everyone' longing.

His days were once lustrous
and evenings a rosy blonde.
When his hope was high
He weaved fanciful visual nights.
How he lavished his liberal hand to
all the treasures that he possessed?

I find his tiny traces in Apollo
or vanishing lunar light.
As I have all praise, less to blame,
I thank god for past every moment,
and love you for thy timely prick,
It was all my choice if I were a failure.

Now I can shun my greed and strife
as you taught me a restful sleep.
I want to wake up for new year morn,
sound in judgement, devoid of wasteful desire.

Singularity of the Plurality

As the eyes blink to face the sun,
Life trembles with the lack of air.
The birth never meets the death
As soul is free but muscle-bound.
One force guides the other,
Two forces work together
but they needn't exist at same place.

The monism nullifies our lives as
nothing that we do, ultimately survives.
No progress or flaws, nothing begins or ends,
World is not like that, world is full of blind fjord,
Never finished, never the same twice,
Lost as we hold, always to be regained.

Perfection is a fallen fruit
between that meaning and the matter.
Our desire to get that supreme state
plasters each aperture by numb ideal of white-
universal refusing to allow division or dispersal.

If man is an image of God, the god disintegrates,
Man is man because once he was a beast.
Man is crazy with resentment, he is dashed
by good hopes or bad dreams against the world,
but is conscious of the joy of things and
the power of going beyond and
above the limits of time

*************************Thanks************************